Native Americans at the Time of the Explorers

BY STEVEN OTFINOSKI

Table of Contents

Pictures To Think About

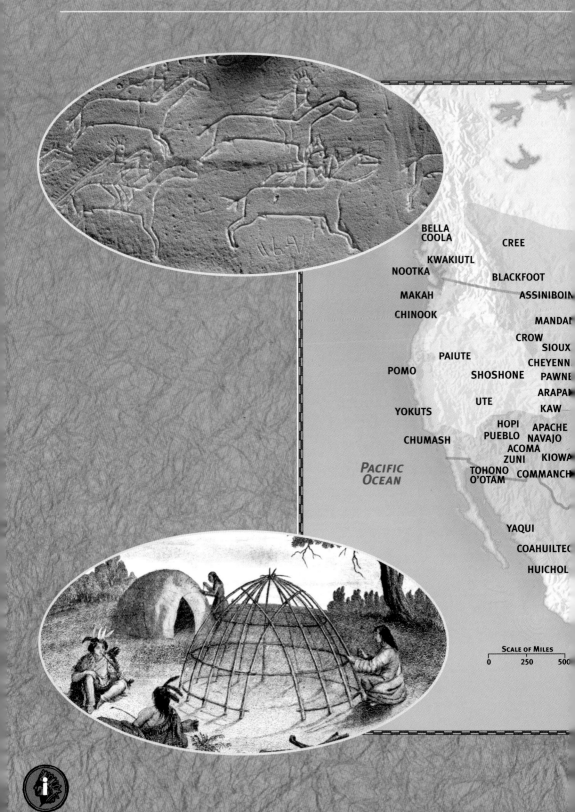

BELLA
COOLA

CREE

KWAKIUTL

NOOTKA

BLACKFOOT

MAKAH

ASSINIBOIN

CHINOOK

MANDAN

CROW

SIOUX

PAIUTE

CHEYENN

POMO

SHOSHONE

PAWNE

ARAPAI

UTE

YOKUTS

KAW

HOPI

APACHE

PUEBLO

NAVAJO

CHUMASH

ACOMA

ZUNI

KIOWA

PACIFIC
OCEAN

TOHONO
O'OTAM

COMMANCH

YAQUI

COAHUILTEC

HUICHOL

SCALE OF MILES

0   250   500

Hudson
Bay

BWA
OJIBWA
MICMAC
L. Superior OTTAWA ALGONKIN PENOBSCOT
IPPEWA HURON
L. Huron
L. Ontario MASSACHUSET
L. Erie
SAUK IROQUOIS LEAGUE
FOX ERIE CAYUGA
WA MIAMI MOHAWK
ILLINOIS DELAWARE ONEIDA
ONONDAGA
SSOURI SHAWNEE SENECA
POWHATAN
AGE
UAPAW YUCHI TUSCARORA
CHICKASAW
DDO
CHOCTAW ATLANTIC
TCHEZ OCEAN

TIMUCUA

CALUSA

Gulf of Mexico

N
W E
S

Words To Think About

Characteristics

- a feast
- guests receive gifts
- ?

potlatch

What do you think the word potlatch means?

Examples

- a wedding
- a birth
- ?

tradition

What do you think the word tradition means?

Latin: *traditio* (handing over)

Latin: *-ion* (the act or process)

tribe

What do you think the word **tribe** means?

What do people in a **tribe** have in common?

What are some Native American **tribes**?

language	?	family roots

Chumash	?	Utes

Introduction

The first European **explorers** found many different people living in North America. Between one and two million Native Americans lived there. They had lived there for at least 19,000 years. Each group had a name.

The first Americans came from Asia. They may have crossed a land bridge to Alaska when the sea was low. They may have followed the animals they hunted to North America.

It's a Fact

About 600 Native American **tribes** were living in North America when the first European explorers arrived. Some of those groups are shown on the map on page 3.

ARCTIC
OCEAN

Gulf of
Alaska

TLINGIT

HAIDA

BELLA
COOLA

KWAKIUTL

NOOTKA

MAKAH

CHINOOK

CREE

Hudson
Bay

BEOTHUK

MICMAC

BLACKFOOT

ASSINIBOINE OJIBWA

OJIBWA

L. Superior

OTTAWA ALGONKIN

PENOBSCOT

MANDAN

CROW

CHIPPEWA

HURON

L. Ontario

MASSACHUSET

PAIUTE

SIOUX

L. Michigan

L. Huron

L. Erie

IROQUOIS LEAGUE

CAYUGA

POMO

CHEYENNE

SHOSHONE

PAWNEE

ARAPAHO

SAUK

FOX

IOWA

ERIE

MIAMI

MOHAWK

ONEIDA

ONONDAGA

DELAWARE

UTE

ILLINOIS

SENECA

YOKUTS

KAW

MISSOURI

SHAWNEE

POWHATAN

CHUMASH

HOPI

PUEBLO

APACHE

NAVAJO

ACOMA

ZUNI

KIOWA

OSAGE

QUAPAW YUCHI

TUSCARORA

COMMANCHE

CHICKASAW

PACIFIC
OCEAN

TOHONO
O'OTAM

CADDO

CHOCTAW

NATCHEZ

ATLANTIC
OCEAN

YAQUI

TIMUCUA

CALUSA

Gulf of Mexico

COAHUILTEC

HUICHOL

Caribbean Sea

Northwest Coast

California

Great Basin

Southwest

Plains

Eastern Woodlands

N

W   E

S

SCALE OF MILES

0   250   500

3

Some Native Americans fished. Others hunted. Some groups gathered nuts, berries, and wild plants. Others farmed. They all depended on the land and the weather.

Sometimes animals died out. Then the people could not hunt those animals for food. Sometimes there was not enough rain. Then people could not grow food. They had to move to a new place where they could find and grow food.

In the early 1500s, the European explorers came. Their arrival changed the way Native Americans lived. Read on to find out more about Native Americans, their lives, and how their world changed.

▼ Navajo pictographs show the arrival of Spaniards on horseback.

Chumash pipe ▲

Solve This

1. The population of Europe in the year 1500 was about 60 million. About 2 million people lived in North America at that time. About how many more people lived in Europe than in North America?

MATH ✓ POINT

What information wasn't needed to solve the problem?

▲ This bowl was made by the Zuni of New Mexico.

The People of California, the Pacific Northwest, and the Great Basin

J uan Rodriguez Cabrillo (WAHN rahd-REE-ges kuh-BREE-yoh) came to what is now California in 1542. He and his crew probably met the Chumash (CHOO-mash). The Chumash were Native Americans who lived in that area of North America.

TLINGIT

BELLA
HAIDA COOLA
CREE

KWAKIUTL
NOOTKA
BLACKFOOT

MAKAH

CHINOOK

PAIUTE
POMO
SHOSHONE

UTE

YOKUTS

HOPI APACHE
CHUMASH PUEBLO NAVAJO
ACOMA
ZUNI
TOHONO
O'OTAM

Solve This

2. There were at least 40 different American Indian groups living in California in Cabrillo's time. There were about 600 American Indian groups in all North America. What fraction of the groups lived in California?

MATH ✓ POINT

What strategy did you use to solve the problem?

▲ A Chumash plank canoe could measure up to 40 feet (12.2 meters).

California: The Chumash

The Chumash lived in villages along the California coast. The Chumash traveled from village to village in long **canoes** (kuh-NOOZ).

The Chumash traded goods. They also hunted and fished. They gathered food, too. Their most important food was the acorn. They ground the nuts into meal. They used the meal to make bread and other foods.

The Spanish settled in the area around 1572. They forced the Chumash to work for them. Many Chumash died from sickness. Over time, the Spanish took the Chumash land for themselves.

It's a Fact

The Chumash made colorful rock paintings of people, animals, and odd shapes. They made paint out of crushed colored rocks mixed with animal fat. The colors they made included bright yellows, burning reds, and icy blues. A feather or strong leaf was used as a brush.

People of the Pacific Northwest

Many tribes lived in what is now Alaska, Washington, Oregon, and northern California. The tribes spoke forty-five different languages.

Most tribes lived along rivers or on the coast. Most of the people fished. Some hunted animals. Others gathered fruit and wild berries.

These people made canoes from tree trunks. They also built wooden **longhouses**.

It rained a lot so they made waterproof clothes from tree **bark**. Others made clothes from animal skins. The clothes kept them warm in cold weather.

Totem Poles

The Northwest Indians had poles carved with totems. Totems represente spirits of their ancestors, the people who came before them. Totems could look like animals or people. Many showed events in a family's history. Families proudly placed their poles in front of their homes.

▲ Totem poles represent spirits of ancestors.

The Tlingit

The Tlingit (TLING-kit) were an important tribe in the Northwest. A few rich families were the village leaders. Those families gave great parties called **potlatches** (PAHT-latch-ehz).

These parties lasted for days. People sang, danced, and feasted. The hosts gave gifts to the guests. The gifts were foods, blankets, or even canoes.

▲ This is a potlatch feast dish. Some dishes were the size of a small canoe.

Great Traders of the Pacific Northwest

The Chinook (shih-NOOK) were known as the great traders of the Northwest. They traded shells, seal oil, and dried fish with other groups.

The Chinook welcomed the first traders from Europe. Soon, the Chinook way of life started to change.

The traders brought diseases that killed the Chinook. Settlers took away their land. Many seals were killed for their fur. Few seals were left to hunt.

It's a Fact

Traders all along the Pacific coast spoke a mixture of English, French, and Chinook. This enabled many different people to do business together.

▼ the Chinook

People of the Great Basin

The Great Basin includes the states of Nevada and Utah. It also includes parts of four other states. The land there is dry. It has few rivers and lakes. It does not rain there often.

The tribes that lived there were gatherers. They ate roots, berries, snakes, grubs, and grasshoppers.

When the Europeans came, they brought horses. Horses changed the lives of Native Americans. The Utes (YOOTS) became raiders and traders. The Shoshone (shuh-SHOH-nee) hunted buffalo.

They Made a Difference

Sacajawea (sa-kuh-juh-WEE-uh) was Shoshone. She traveled with explorers Lewis and Clark. Together, they traveled from the Missouri River to the Columbia River and the Pacific Ocean, and back. Sacajawea got her people to give the explorers horses. She used **sign language** to speak to the people of other tribes. Sacajawea played a key role in making the trip successful.

◀ Some of these stone carvings may be the work of the Shoshone.

The People of the Southwest

The Pueblo (PWEH-bloh) people lived in the area around Santa Fe (SAN-tuh FAY), New Mexico. Spanish settlers went there in 1600. The Spanish took over the land and ruled the Pueblo for eighty years. The Spanish were harsh rulers.

The Pueblo fought back. One hot August day, they killed more than 400 Spanish. The Pueblo remained free until 1692.

PAIUTE
SHOSHONE
UTE
HOPI APACHE
PUEBLO NAVAJO
ACOMA
ZUNI
TOHONO
O'OTAM
YAQUI
COAHUILTEC
HUICHOL

Solve This

3. The Spanish fled Santa Fe for El Paso, Texas, after the Pueblo attack. They came back in 1692. How many years after the attack did they return?

MATH ✓ POINT

What information did you use to solve this problem?

Harsh Land and Sky-High Homes

The land of the Southwest is hot and dry. Early farmers like the Anasazi (ah-nuh-SAH-zee) still found ways to bring water to dry places. They were able to grow enough food to feed many people. They grew corn, beans, and squash.

Many people lived in **pueblos** (PWEH-blohz). Each pueblo had many apartments. Hundreds of people might live in one pueblo.

These homes were made of adobe (uh-DOH-bee). Adobe is brick made of clay and straw.

Solve This

4. If an average summer temperature in the Southwest is 105°F, what would it be in Celsius? (To change Fahrenheit to Celsius, subtract 32. Then multiply by 5 and divide by 9. Round answer to nearest whole number.)

MATH ✓ POINT

How did you check your work?

The Acoma Pueblo is the oldest lived-in community in the United States. It is often called Sky City.

The Peaceful Ones

One group of Pueblo people was the Hopi (HOH-pee). The name means "peaceful ones." The Hopi lived in homes that were three stories high. The Hopi used ladders to climb from house to house.

The homes were connected in long rows.

The Hopi grew corn, beans, and squash. They marked their gardens with rocks. They painted symbols on the rocks. The symbols gave hints on how to grow things.

Kachinas—Spirits of the Dead

Kachinas (kuh-CHEE-nuz) were part of the Hopi religion. Kachinas were spirits of the dead. During religious ceremonies, Hopi men dressed as kachinas. They took the form of animals, plants, and humans. They danced to bring rain or a full harvest. There were about 250 different kachinas, all with special powers.

The Navajo

The Navajo (NA-vuh-hoh) settled in the Southwest in about 1025. The Navajo were hunters and gatherers. They lived in homes called hogans (HOH-gahnz). Hogans were shaped like domes.

The Navajo raided the Hopi and other Pueblo people. They took food, goods, and slaves. The Navajo also took on many Pueblo **traditions** (truh-DIH-shunz). These traditions included masked dancing, sand painting, and weaving.

▲ Navajo blankets were special. Some were very tightly woven. Water could not get through them.

The Spanish arrived in the 1600s. They brought sheep. Soon many Navajo became shepherds.

▲ The wooden frame of a Navajo hogan was covered with bark and earth. The doorway always faced east.

The People of the Great Plains

Early people of the Great Plains hunted buffalo. They would creep up on a herd. Then they would shout and scare the animals. The animals would run over the cliffs and die.

Around 1680, the Spanish came with horses. The people of the Great Plains had never seen horses. At first, they thought the rider and horse were one person. But soon, the Plains Indians learned to ride horses. This changed how they hunted.

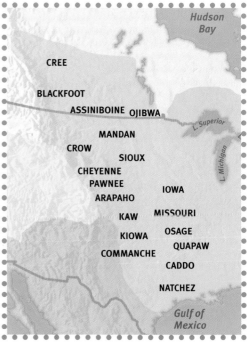

CREE
BLACKFOOT
ASSINIBOINE OJIBWA
MANDAN
CROW
SIOUX
CHEYENNE
PAWNEE
ARAPAHO
KAW
KIOWA
COMMANCHE
IOWA
MISSOURI
OSAGE
QUAPAW
CADDO
NATCHEZ
Hudson Bay
L. Superior
L. Michigan
Gulf of Mexico

▲ The Great Plains are from the Mississippi River to the Rocky Mountains, and from Texas to Canada.

▼ The Plains Indians hunted buffalo on foot for hundreds of years.

16

Hunters on horseback could follow the buffalo herds. Families moved often. They lived in **tepees** (TEE-peez). Tepees were easy to set up and take down. Wooden poles were tied in a V shape. Then animal skins were wrapped around the poles.

When the hunters moved, the skins were tied across the tepee frame. A horse or dog pulled the load. Sometimes children or the sick rode on top of the load.

The Useful Buffalo

The people of the Western Plains used every part of the buffalo. They used the skin to make their tepees, and for clothing and blankets. They made tools from the bones and horns. The animal's hair was twisted into rope. Even the buffalo's tail was used as a fly swatter!

Each tribe spoke its own language. People used sign language to talk to people in other tribes.

▼ The travois (truh-VOY) was made from the tepee frame. A horse or dog pulled it. The wide end dragged on the ground.

Lords of the Southern Plains

The Comanche (kuh-MAN-chee) lived in what is now Wyoming. The Comanche hunted buffalo. They used the buffalo hides for clothes, food, and shelter. They also lived in tepees made from the hides.

When the Comanche got horses, they followed the buffalo herds. They also raided other tribes.

The Comanche had many groups. A chief led each group. The chiefs met to make rules and decisions. The Comanche built a powerful **nation**. They were called the "Lords of the Southern Plains."

Myth or Reality?

Coronado Looks for Gold

Spanish explorer Francisco de Coronado (frun-SIS-koh DUH kor-uh-NAH-doh) searched the Southwest for seven cities of gold. American Indians told him about gold at the city of Quivira (KEY-vee-rah). It was across the Great Plains, in what is now Kansas. Quivira turned out to be a simple Wichita village. Did the seven cities of gold really exist? No. But, if Coronado had gone further west, he just might have found gold in California.

Farmers and Hunters

The Eastern Great Plains were good for growing crops. The Wichita (WIH-chih-tau) and Omaha (OH-muh-hah) people farmed there in spring and fall. In summer and winter they hunted buffalo on the plains.

The Omaha people ▶ lived in earth lodges.

Solve This

5. The prairie grass that Coronado passed through in the Great Plains grew up to 8 feet (2.4 meters) tall. If Coronado was about 5 feet, 8 inches tall (1.7 meters), how much taller was the grass than Coronado?

MATH ✔ POINT

What strategy did you use to solve the problem?

▼ Great Plains Indians hunted buffalo on horseback.

The People of the Eastern Woodlands

The Algonquian (al-GAHN-kwee-uhn) and the Iroquois (EER-uh-kwoi) were bitter enemies. In 1609, French explorer Samuel de Champlain (dih sham-PLANE) offered to help the Algonquian. Champlain and the Algonquian formed a war party. Together they fought the Iroquois.

The French had muskets. They killed many Iroquois.

The Iroquois never forgot that day. The French became their enemy. Later, during the French and Indian War, the Iroquois joined the English. They fought against the French.

BEOTHUK

MICMAC

OJIBWA

L. Superior OTTAWA ALGONKIN PENOBSCOT

HURON

CHIPPEWA

L. Huron

L. Ontario

MASSACHUSET

SAUK

L. Michigan

L. Erie

IROQUOIS LEAGUE

FOX ERIE CAYUGA

MIAMI MOHAWK

DELAWARE ONEIDA

ILLINOIS ONONDAGA

SHAWNEE POWHATAN SENECA

YUCHI TUSCARORA

CHICKASAW

CADDO ATLANTIC

CHOCTAW OCEAN

NATCHEZ

TIMUCUA

Gulf of Mexico CALUSA

The eastern third of the United States was filled with forest.

Life in the Woodlands

The people of the Eastern Woodlands lived on land that had rich natural resources. The land had good soil. The forests were filled with animals, nuts, and berries. The rivers and oceans held plenty of fish. People hunted, fished, and farmed. They grew squash, corn, beans, and wild rice.

In the north, many people lived in longhouses made of wood poles and bark. These homes kept the people warm in the winter. In the south, it was hot. People lived in homes without walls.

It's a Fact

Sacred Iroquois masks were made of corn husks. At the start of the new year, members of the secret Husk Face Society wore the masks. They danced to ask the spirits for a good harvest.

▼ Many longhouses were between 100 and 200 feet long (30.5 and 61 meters). The ceremonial longhouse often was longer.

The Five Nations of the Iroquois

The Iroquois were one of the most powerful groups in this area. The tribes lived far apart. They often fought with each other. They also knew they needed to work together.

In 1570, five groups of tribes, or nations, joined together. They formed a government. It was called the Iroquois League (LEEG). The League was formed to try to end the fighting among the tribes. All five nations had to agree on each decision. The U.S. Constitution uses ideas from the Iroquois League.

Solve This

6. Use the scale on the map to figure out the distance from the southwest corner of the Iroquois Nation to the northeast corner. About how many miles is it? How many kilometers? Then figure out the distance across the bottom from west to east.

MATH ✔ POINT

Did it help to estimate your answer? Why or why not?

Land of the Iroquois

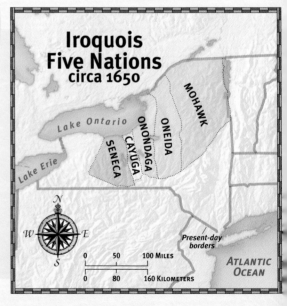

Iroquois
Five Nations
circa 1650

Lake Ontario

MOHAWK
ONEIDA
ONONDAGA
CAYUGA
SENECA

Lake Erie

N
W — E
S

Present-day borders

0   50   100 MILES
0   80   160 KILOMETERS

ATLANTIC OCEAN

The Algonquian

The Algonquian lived in the northern part of the Woodlands. They lived in villages along the Atlantic coast. The Algonquian farmed, hunted and gathered, and fished. They were among the first people to meet the European explorers.

The European explorers introduced the Algonquian to horses and metal tools. The Algonquian shared corn, pumpkins, cranberries, shellfish, and other foods with the explorers.

▼ Algonquian wigwams (WIHG-wahmz) were made of small trees bent and tied together. They were covered by birch-bark strips sewn together.

The Narragansett

The Narragansett (nair-uh-GAN-set) lived in what is now Rhode Island. They were a powerful tribe. In the winter, the Narragansett lived in long homes. In the summer, they lived near the coast.

In 1524, Giovanni da Verrazzano (joh-VAH-nee duh vair-uh-ZAH-noh) explored the coast of North America. He was looking for a route to Asia. He stopped in Rhode Island to give his men a rest. The Narragansett met them and took care of them.

Primary Source

In his report to the king of France, Verrazzano wrote about the Narragansett, " . . . their manner is sweet and gentle." His journals have the earliest information about the people who lived in the area.

▲ The Narragansett welcomed Giovanni da Verrazzano to Rhode Island.

Historical Perspective

The Lost Colony of Roanoke

In 1587, 117 English settlers arrived on Roanoke (ROH-uh-noke) Island. Roanoke Island is part of present-day North Carolina. When settlers ran low on supplies, John White returned to England. He brought samples of tobacco, corn, and other local products. Two friendly Indians also sailed with him.

They couldn't return for three years. But when they did come back, the colony was empty. "CRO" was carved in a tree. Those first settlers were never heard from again.

▲ Ads like this invited English people to settle in North America.

Solve This

7. In 1513, Juan Ponce de León (WAHN PAHN-suh DUH LEE-one) explored Florida and met the Timucua. There, in 1565, other explorers founded St. Augustine (ah-GUH-steen). How long was this after Ponce de León first arrived in Florida?

The Timucua

The Timucua (TEE-moo-kwah) lived in what is now northern Florida. They lived in villages.

Their homes were round houses. The chief lived in the middle of the village. A high log wall surrounded each village. The wall kept the village safe.

The Timucua farmed, fished, and hunted. They stored their food so they could share it in hard times. They used canoes to travel and trade.

MATH ✔ POI

What information did you use to solve the problem?

◀ This is John White's painting of a Timucua archer. The Timucua tattooed their bodies to show their power and position.

So That's Where It Comes From!

Many words in the English language come from around the world. But here are some words that come from American Indians.

HOMINY
(HAH-mih-nee)
corn without the shiny covering. *Hominy* is an Algonquian word. The Algonquian were Eastern Woodlands Indians.

POWWOW
(POW-wow)
an American Indian ceremony or social gathering. *Powwow* is a Narragansett word.

MOCCASINS
(MAH-kuh-sinz)
soft shoes without heels. *Moccasin* is a Narragansett word. The Narragansett were Eastern Woodlands Indians.

RACCOON
(ra-KOON)
a small night animal. It has a black mask, gray fur, and a bushy, ringed tail. *Raccoon* is an Algonquian word.

✔POINT

Read More About It

Find out about the Native Americans that lived in or near where you live today. How many places in your state have Native American names? Share your information with classmates.

Conclusion

Before Europeans arrived in North America, Native Americans lived in many different ways. Some hunted animals. Some gathered wild plants and berries. Others fished in the oceans and lakes. Many also farmed. Each tribe lived off the land.

Then the explorers came. Life changed for the tribes. They learned to do new things. They rode horses. They raised sheep. They hunted with guns. The Europeans learned many new things from the Native Americans, too.

▲ Shoshone painting on buffalo hide

Use the chart below to talk about the early Native Americans. How did they live? How did their lives change after the Europeans arrived? What stayed the same? Share your thoughts with the class.

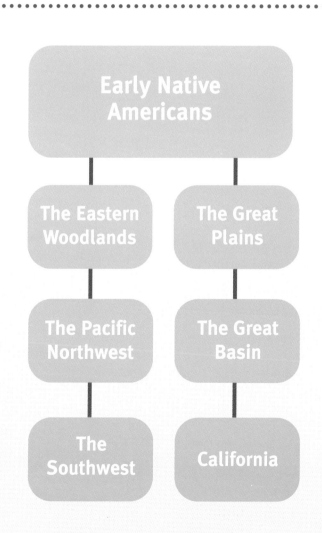

Solve This
Answers

1. PAGE 5
58 million
60,000,000 – 2,000,000
= 58,000,000
MATH CHECKPOINT
The date, 1500, is not needed.

2. PAGE 6
1/15
MATH CHECKPOINT
Reduce the fraction 40/600 to lowest terms.

3. PAGE 12
12 years
MATH CHECKPOINT
According to the text, the Spaniards ruled the Pueblo people for 80 years, from 1600–1680. The Spaniards fled and returned in 1692. 1692 – 1680 = 12.

4. PAGE 13
41°C (40.55°C rounded up)
MATH CHECKPOINT
To check work, multiply
40.55 x 9 = 364.95 ÷ 5
= 72.99 + 32 = 104.99°F.
Rounded up, it equals 105°F.

5. PAGE 19
The grass was 28 inches (.7 meters) taller than Coronado.

MATH CHECKPOINT
8 feet is 96 inches, since there are 12 inches to one foot. 12 x 8 = 96.
5 feet, 8 inches is 68 inches. 5 x 12 = 60 + 8 = 68. 96 – 68 = 28. (2.4 meters – 1.7 meters = .7 meters)

6. PAGE 22
Southwest to northeast corners:
About 280 miles; 451 km
(280 x 1.6093 = 450.60)
West to east:
About 225 miles; 362 km
(225 x 1.6093 = 362.09)
MATH CHECKPOINT
No. You need to use the scale of miles and measure.

7. PAGE 26
52 years
1565 – 1513 = 52
MATH CHECKPOINT
You need the date that Ponce de Leon came to Florida the first time: 1513. You need the date St. Augustine was founded: 1565.

Glossary

bark   (BARK) the tough outside covering of a tree's trunk and branches (page 8)

canoe   (kuh-NOO) a light, narrow boat made from wood; it has sharp ends and is moved by paddles (page 7)

explorer   (ik-SPLOR-er) a person who goes to find out about a place (page 2)

kachina   (kuh-CHEE-nuh) over 200 different spirits which the Pueblo people honored; dolls are carved to stand for the spirits (page 14)

longhouse   (LAUNG-hows) a long, wooden building in which several families live together (page 8)

nation   (NAY-shun) group of Native American tribes who share the same language and family roots, customs, and land (page 18)

potlatch   (PAHT-lach) a feast, given by Northwest tribes, where guests receive goods that were worth a lot; a potlatch often celebrated important events such as a birth, a wedding, or a death (page 9)

pueblo   (PWEH-bloh) a Spanish word that means "village," it is a group of houses next to or on top of each other (page 13)

sign language   (SINE LAN-gwij) speaking through hand movements instead of the voice (page 11)

tepee   (TEE-pee) the skin-covered, V-shaped shelters of the Plains Indians (page 17)

tradition   (truh-DIH-shuhn) a way of doing something that is passed on from parents to children (page 15)

tribe   (TRIBE) a group of people who share the same language, customs, land, and family roots (page 2)

Index